I0428198

LEAD ME, FOLLOW ME, OR GET OUT OF MY WAY: RETHINKING AND REFINING THE CIVIL-MILITARY RELATIONSHIP

Introduction.

The constitutional linchpins of human rights — most notably, the four key elements: regular elections, habeas corpus, freedom of expression, and civilian control of the military — ensure that the people remain sovereign in a democratic society by allowing them to hold governments accountable. These instruments work to prevent arbitrariness in government. They enable the people to speak and ensure that their leaders will hear. The instruments imply, too, that the government will respond appropriately with remedies for valid complaints. Without any one of these constitutional linchpins, substantive human rights cannot be enforced. In such circumstances, governments may still recognize the legitimate claims of individuals — but only by grace, not by right.

Each of these elements is necessary to ensure that the full host of human rights claims is protected.[1] The significance of each particular element has been examined at length elsewhere. For instance, much has been written about the critical roles that regular elections and the freedom of expression play in promoting responsive government. Likewise, U.S. policies and practices for detaining alleged terrorists have, over the past 10 years, given the study of *habeas corpus* a tremendous boost. But the fourth element, civilian control of the military, remains less developed.[2] This monograph explores U.S. civil-military relations and their connection to human rights, taking two impor-

1

tant new books as a prompt and springboard for further exploration.

This monograph begins by explaining why robust civil-military relations matter. Without meaningful and reliable civilian control of the military, governments lose some measure of control over the destiny of their nations. In extreme circumstances, the lack of such control can even lead to an overthrow of government. Part I, *A More Perfect Military: How the Constitution Can Make Our Military Stronger*, by law professor Diane Mazur, examines the constitutional jurisprudence that has reshaped U.S. civil-military relations over the past 4 decades. Her carefully documented argument maintains that since the Vietnam era, the U.S. Supreme Court has hewn the Armed Forces from the general society in order to create a separate—and more socially conservative—sphere. Part II, *The Decline and Fall of the American Republic*, by constitutional scholar Bruce Ackerman, is a wise and wide-ranging book that argues that the nation's polity is in decline and that the increasingly politicized armed forces may ultimately lead to a coup. Part III asks where we go from here.

The important books under consideration attribute a thinning of the civilian control over the military to legal and political decisions made over the past 30 years. They explain some of the most important implications of this transformation, and offer sensible proposals about how to improve the critical military-civilian relationship for the sake of enhancing the effectiveness of our Armed Forces and the vitality of our republic. But neither work examines the evolving nature of great-power politics since the end of the Cold War, the effects new technologies have on long-standing distinctions and borders, or the relative rise of nonstate actors including al Qaeda — three sets of exogenous factors that inevitably drive changes in the civil-military relationship. So, in the end, these books point to the need for a more ambitious enterprise: a complete re-examination of the relationship between force and society in the 21st century.

Before discussing the books, a brief discussion of the civil-military relationship is required. The astonishing events of the Arab Spring in 2011 illuminate important truths about the nature of governments and governance. Most notably, they demonstrated that in order to rule, civilian leadership must exercise consistent and reliable control over the state's security apparatus. In the case of repressive regimes, stability may not be normatively desirable, but it remains a significant factor nonetheless. Without the ability to control the army, almost any regime will fall. This lesson may seem obvious or axiomatic, but it bears repeating and illustrating. The Tunisian military's refusal to support the long-standing regime in the face of a popular uprising condemned President Zine El Abidine Ben Ali to a rapid fall from power.[3] Shortly thereafter, the world watched anxiously to see whether the Egyptian military would remain loyal to the regime of President Hosni Mubarak or shift the balance of power to the protesters crowding Cairo's Tahrir Square. Much like its counterparts in Tunisia, the Egyptian military tried to appear an honest broker, effectively denying support to the president and thus ensuring the protesters the space in which to give effect to their revolution.[4] Months after Mubarak fled Cairo, the military continues to exercise power, running the interim government.[5]

In contrast, the armed forces of Bahrain and Syria have thus far remained mostly obedient to their governments, which in turn have, to date, survived.[6] The case of Libya illustrates a third way. The Libyan military was split on supporting the regime of Muammar Muhammad el-Qaddafi, resulting in a bitter and hotly fought civil war.[7] In every instance in which the military has fully supported the government, the government survived. Where the military turned against the national leadership, the government fell. Where the military has vacillated, violent conflict and political indeterminacy ensued.

This brief sketch of Arab Spring leads to several axiomatic observations that certainly apply in the Muslim world and possibly elsewhere. When a nation's armed forces take orders from the civilian leadership, the government has a good chance of retaining power. When the military is not absolutely obedient, the regime's ability to govern is significantly diminished. When the military defects, a change in leadership invariably results. The events of Arab Spring offer a timely and poignant reminder of the roles that armed forces can play in the life and death of a state. This critical fact has rarely been commented on with regard to the United States, but it nevertheless remains very real. When the government no longer exercises a monopoly on the use of large-scale violence, the regime's effectiveness and longevity become less certain. This lesson might seem self-evident, but it is worth spelling out because of its momentous implications.

Of course, Arab Spring affected very different kinds of countries and therefore offers limited value for a study of the United States. The affected countries were not functional democracies with robust rule-of-law systems and traditions of ordered liberty. Instead, they were run by people who had risen to power through the ranks of the armed services or taken power themselves through military means. Their institutions of civil society were meager. Their cultures were plagued by discontent, particularly among the vast portion of society that is young and desperately underemployed. The armed forces themselves were more oriented toward state security roles than those required for fighting wars against other states. This orientation may have made the militaries more likely to make autonomous decisions about whether to support their governments. In all these ways and more, the countries directly affected by Arab Spring differ significantly from the United States. Nevertheless, the basic point remains valid: If a country's leadership cannot rely on the military for complete and unfailing support of its policies, then the range of policies its political leaders can pursue is limited by the military and not by political leadership.

Effective civilian control of the military, therefore, is an unheralded linchpin of human rights. Just as an actual linchpin secures a wheel to the axle, civilian control of the military ensures that the armed forces do not spin off or diverge from the policies of the constituted governments. U.S. military officers take an oath of office to support and defend the Constitution.[8] That oath articulates and embodies the principal obligations of officers. Without the loyalty commanded by that oath, the rights of civilians are not fully guaranteed, even though they may be more or less respected as a matter of policy or habit. Therefore, civilian control is necessary to: (1) ensure representative government and, consequently, almost every other human right; (2) prevent militarization of civil society and the civilianization of the military; and, (3) ensure effective barriers between the law, norms, and privileges of war and those of civil society.

The 2011 U.S. *National Military Strategy* provides a crisp statement of the American tradition of civilian control over the military and its immediate implications:

> We [the Joint Forces] will maintain the trust and confidence of our elected leaders and the public by providing frank, professional military advice; being good stewards of public resources; and vigorously executing lawful orders. The military's adherence to the ideals comprised in our Constitution is a profound example for other nations. We will continue to affirm the foundational values in our oath: civilian control of the military remains a core principle of our Republic and we will preserve it. We will remain an apolitical institution and sustain this position at all costs.[9]

Inclusion of this statement represents a welcome change from the previous *National Military Strategy*, from which it was absent.[10]

To drive the point home, Admiral Michael Mullen, then outgoing Chairman of the Joint Chiefs, recently explained this principle to a new generation of officers, notably at the Class of 2011 Commencement ceremony at the U.S. Military Academy at West Point, NY:

> I'm going to ask you to remember that you are citizens first and foremost. This great republic of ours was founded on some pretty simple ideas — simple but enduring. And one of them is that the people, through their elected representatives, will, as the Constitution stipulates, raise an army and maintain a navy. The people will determine the course the military steers, the skills we perfect, the wars we fight. The people reign supreme. We answer to them. We are therefore — and must remain — a neutral instrument of the state, accountable to our civilian leaders no matter which political party holds sway.[11]

Admiral Mullen's account is notable because he included it in his valedictory commencement address.[12] Why did he feel compelled to remind the cadets that they remain citizens, and that they must serve as neutral instruments of state? What factors moved him to speak these most fundamental concepts as if there was an urgent need to express them at this particular time? Constitutional law scholars Diane H. Mazur and Bruce Ackerman provide some insights to these questions.

A Separate Sphere.

Diane H. Mazur is one of the rare women who has served as a military officer and then gone on to teach full time in an American law school.[13] As a young Air Force captain, she had served as an aircraft-maintenance and then a munitions-maintenance officer before attending law school. Following graduation, she practiced law for a few years and then joined the faculty of the University of Florida Levin College of Law. Since the mid-1990s, Mazur has written extensively on civil-military relations, focusing particularly on sexual minorities in the military and the related "Don't ask, don't tell" policy controversies. She has also written a number of policy studies for the Palm Center, a research institute focusing on gender, sexuality, and the military, where she serves as Legal Co-Director. Her new book, *A More Perfect Military: How the Constitution Can Make Our Military Stronger*, brings together a career's worth of military, scholarly, and advocacy work in one powerful argument.

The title of this book plays on the Preamble of the U.S. Constitution nicely to convey the thesis—"that the military is most healthy when it respects constitutional values."[14] Mazur argues that "[u]nfortunately, since the end of the Vietnam draft, our civilian branches of government—the President, Congress, and the courts—have been trying to distance the military from the Constitution. They assume that constitutional values get in the way of military effectiveness, but that's not true."[15] Mazur sets out to cut through the cant and "change all the rules that limit the way we talk about the military."[16] Unlike Bruce Ackerman, whose new book will be discussed below, Mazur does not focus on the constitutional implications of a strained civil-military relationship. Recognizing the same general phenomenon, Ackerman argues that this relationship might lead to some sort of military intervention or coup in the United States. Mazur goes in a different direction. She believes that our "confidence that the military will never engage in a coup against civilian government, or anything even remotely close to a coup" should not confuse us into believing that civil-military relations are good.[17] Mazur believes that Congress and especially the judiciary have been effectively working to distinquish the members of the Armed Services from the general population, to the detriment of civil-military relations and, ultimately, to the vibrancy of the Armed Forces. Mazur's book argues for tearing down the recently constructed legal walls that have segregated the Armed Forces from the rest of society. Doing so will, she argues, endow the nation with a more robust force, one more capable of defending the Constitution against all enemies, foreign and domestic.[18]

At the heart of Mazur's book is the claim that over the past 4 decades, conservative lawmakers and judges have carved out a separate sphere for the military. In it, they have promoted conservative social values without heed to the modern constitutional protections for individuals. To insulate the Armed Forces from the social progress that has been transforming civilian society, they have created strong rhetorical and legal barriers that prevent the questioning of military choices. To make this argument, Mazur draws widely on recent American history, including such notable episodes as the 1991 Tailhook Scandal, the formation of the "Don't ask, don't tell" policy, and the abuse of detainees at Abu Ghraib early in the Second Gulf War.[19] But most critically and innovatively, she examines a strand of the Supreme Court jurisprudence of William Rehnquist.[20] Mazur argues that Justice Rehnquist created circumstances in which "military society could serve as a safe harbor from the usual constitutional expectations . . . [and] could be used to validate and reinforce socially conservative viewpoints."[21] She asserts that Rehnquist revolutionized American civil-military relations for the purpose of promoting his conservative social values.

Mazur's story opens with Rehnquist as a recent Stanford Law School graduate clerking for Justice Robert H. Jackson. In 1953, the Supreme Court heard *Orloff v. Willoughby*, a low-profile case about a doctor challenging the Army's decisions to draft him under the Doctors' Draft Act of 1948 and then not to commission him as a medical officer, presumably because of his unwillingness to deny that he was a Communist.[22] Orloff had argued that because he could be drafted only on account of his being a doctor, the Army must either commission him as a medical officer or discharge him.

The Supreme Court held otherwise, ruling for the Army. Justice Jackson wrote:

We know that from top to bottom of the Army, the complaint is often made, and sometimes with justification, that there is discrimination, favoritism, or other objectionable handling of men. But judges are not given the task of running the Army. The responsibility for setting up channels through which such grievances can be considered and fairly settled rests upon the Congress and upon the President of the United States and his subordinates. *The military constitutes a specialized community governed by a separate discipline from that of the civilian.* [Emphasis added.] Orderly government requires that the judiciary be as scrupulous not to interfere with legitimate Army matters as the Army must be scrupulous not to intervene in judicial matters.[23]

Mazur agrees with the decision to uphold the Army's authority to self-regulate. She goes on to speculate that William Rehnquist may have even drafted this key passage of Justice Jackson's decision.[24] After all, we know that young Rehnquist had drafted a memo to Justice Jackson, then considering *Brown v. Board of Education*, that "*Plessy v. Ferguson* was right and should be re-affirmed."[25] Clearly, he was willing to share his conservative views with Justice Jackson (who had been appointed to the bench by Franklin D. Roosevelt), intending to see them written into the court's opinions. Moreover, Mazur notes that Rehnquist was "preoccupied with the question of the judiciary's proper posture towards the military."[26] In any event, the Korean War-era *Orloff* decision achieved a curious form of momentum during the more politically contentious war that followed.

Joining the Supreme Court in his own right in 1972, Justice Rehnquist set out "to push the military outside our nation's constitutional fold and weaken its connection to civilian courts and civilian law" in a pair of early cases dealing with some of the day's most hotly debated issues.[27] In late-October 1969, John Flower had been ordered off Fort Sam Houston, TX, for distributing anti-war fliers.[28] Six weeks later he returned and was arrested for being on an otherwise open military post and for "distributing handbill invitations for a 'Town meeting' on the Vietnam War."[29] The District Court convicted Flower of unlawfully entering military property and sentenced him to 6 months in prison.[30] The Supreme Court overturned the conviction, holding that "[o]ne who is rightfully on a street which the state has left open to the public carries with him there as elsewhere, the constitutional right to express his views in an orderly fashion."[31] Joined by Chief Justice Warren Burger, Rehnquist dissented:

> Simply because some activities and individuals are allowed on government property does not require the abandonment of otherwise allowable restrictions on its use. . . .[T]he unique requirements of military morale and security may well necessitate control over certain persons and activities on the base, even while normal traffic flow through the area can be tolerated.[32]

Whereas governmental decisions to limit free speech would usually be subject to strict scrutiny, Rehnquist would not even inquire into the legitimacy of those restrictions when applied by the Army. He would not ask for—let alone weigh—their burdens against the benefits to morale and security. He would defer unquestioningly to the military's decision.[33]

The young justice extended this position 2 years later in a more high-profile equal-protection case, *Frontiero v. Richardson*.[34] In this case, Air Force Lieutenant Sharron Frontiero challenged the military's policy of giving all married men extra housing and medical

11

benefits while requiring married women seeking these benefits to prove that their husbands were dependent upon them.[35] In an opinion authored by Justice William Brennan, the court held that classifications based on sex should be subject to strict scrutiny. He found that the Air Force's rationale for this differential treatment, which rested on "administrative convenience," could not stand up to such scrutiny.[36] In Justice Brennan's trenchant words, there "can be no doubt that 'administrative convenience' is not a shibboleth, the mere recitation of which dictates constitutionality."[37] Rehnquist dissented from Brennan's opinion, elevating distinctions based on sex to the same protected status as race, alienage, and national origin.[38] "In determining the constitutionality of the statutory scheme that plaintiffs attack, [he would merely] ask whether the classification established in the legislation is reasonable and not arbitrary and whether there is a rational connection between the classification and a legitimate governmental end."[39] Mazur attributes this position to Rehnquist's willingness to make Frontiero prove that the claim of administrative convenience by the U.S. Department of Defense (DoD) did not exist.[40] Here the record is very thin;[41] perhaps Rehnquist took this position because of an unwillingness to elevate the level of scrutiny for sex-based distinctions rather than out of deference to the military.

If Rehnquist spoke quietly and perhaps ambiguously in *Frontiero*, he came out roaring in three landmark cases that followed the end of military conscription in 1973, *Parker v. Levy* in 1974, *Rostker v. Goldberg* in 1981, and *Goldman v. Weinberger* in 1986.[42] With these three decisions, Rehnquist led the charge to revolutionize the relationship between military and civilian society.[43] According to Mazur, his "opinions would build [a] wedge on a foundation of four troubling principles" that have come increasingly to define the civil-military relationship in today's United States.[44]

> The military should be portrayed as distant, remote, and separate from civilian society. The more different the military is from the civilian society it serves, the less justification there might be for holding the military to the expectations of civilian law.

> The military should be viewed as morally superior to civilian society and civilian government, and military values should be elevated above constitutional values. If military values were morally superior to constitutional values, it would be much easier to disregard the Constitution when its protections appeared to conflict with assertions of military necessity.

> Civilians should be encouraged to withdraw from active participation in civil-military relations and civilian control of the military and to see themselves as unqualified and undeserving to question assertions of military necessity. Service members should be encouraged to resent civilians, civilian society, and civilian influence over the military.

> Judges, courts, and other institutions of law should be reluctant to insert themselves in legal controversies involving the military, creating a vacuum that could be filled by political partisanship and allegiance.[45]

Mazur argues that all this has come to pass, with harmful effects on the military and the republic. To make this argument, she offers a provocative account of Supreme Court decisions affecting the civil-military relationship.

Rehnquist launched this revolution in *Parker v. Levy*, which ought to have been a simple case. In 1966, the "Hawkeye Pierce" of the Vietnam War, Army Captain Howard Levy, started to tell lower-ranking personnel that the war was immoral and that black soldiers were being discriminated against by being "given all the hazardous duty . . . [and that if he] were a colored soldier [he] would refuse to go to Viet Nam and . . . refuse to fight."[46] Not surprisingly, Levy was court-martialed and convicted of conduct unbecoming an officer and for acts that "prejudice . . . good order and discipline in the armed forces."[47] Nor was it remarkable that the Supreme Court upheld the convictions, finding that the charged provisions of the Uniform Code of Military Justice were neither unconstitutionally vague nor overbroad.

The important part of the *Parker v. Levy* story that Mazur reveals is how Rehnquist misrepresented the earlier *Orloff* decision to establish the proposition "that the military should be seen as distant, remote, and separate from civilian society."[48] To do so, he mischaracterized Justice Jackson's *dictum* discussed briefly above: "The military constitutes a specialized community governed by a separate discipline from that of the civilian."[49] Jackson had been referring to the military justice system, but Rehnquist twisted the words to imply that the military was necessarily a society separate and apart from civilian society.[50] He offered what became a self-fulfilling argument. The military in which Captain Levy served had been highly representative of American society in general. Soldiers were not relegated to lifetimes on remote outposts on the frontier as they had been in the century preceding World War II. Instead, conscripts and career soldiers lived within American society. Until the Supreme Court handed down its decision in *Parker v. Levy* in 1974, America's soldiers generally enjoyed all of the freedoms guaranteed by the First Amendment, without admonishment that the exercise of those freedoms was inconsistent with good order and discipline.[51] The *Parker* decision started a process of walling the Armed Forces off from the rest of American society by cutting back their freedom of speech.

In the 1981 case of *Rostker v. Goldberg*, Justice Rehnquist found his opportunity to harden the wall he was drawing around the military. In 1979, President Jimmy Carter had responded to the Soviet invasion of Afghanistan by reinstating draft registration. Contrary to the President's wish to register women as well, Congress authorized funds sufficient only to register eligible men.[52] The Goldberg plaintiffs complained that the process violated the equal protection guarantees of men and women.[53] Mazur explains that the court should have found this an exceedingly difficult case for introducing heightened deference to military decisionmaking.[54] First, unlike previous cases that had generally decided the claims of one person or a small number of people, this case affected all American women between the ages of 18 and 26. Because so many people were affected, it is hard to pass the policy choice off as mere administrative convenience. Second, previous cases had involved the review of decisions made by the military; here, Goldberg was challenging a congressional decision. So the deference here was really to Congress. There is no special deference to Congress. Congress passes all laws, so the ordinary standards of respect among branches should automatically apply. Third, in previous cases, the Court had decided to defer to the military. In this case, the military services had requested funds to register women, too; it was Congress that refused to make the authorization. So the Supreme Court disregarded the military perspective.

Despite these perplexing circumstances, Rehnquist held that "the Constitution itself requires . . . deference to congressional choice."[55] Mazur argues that Rehnquist deferred to the will of Congress over that of the military on this military personnel issue because Congress was seeking to implement its view about the proper role for women in society.[56] This is vexing because in the rest of society, the Constitution specifically did not defer to decisions to make distinctions based on sex. It viewed such distinctions as presumptively unlawful.[57] With the ruling in *Goldberg*, Rehnquist was able to promote a social agenda that used the military as the means to achieve a nonmilitary end. When the military wanted to discriminate in ways that promoted conservative social values, the Rehnquist Court deferred to the military. When Congress wanted to use the military to discriminate, Rehnquist would lead the court to defer to Congress, even against the views of the DoD on a personnel question.

In the final case of this post-draft trilogy, *Goldman v. Weinberger*, Rehnquist further bolstered his wall.[58] S. Simcha Goldman was a clinical psychologist serving as an Air Force officer. As an Orthodox rabbi, he was required by his faith to cover his head. After his superior officer ordered him to remove his yarmulke, Captain Goldman sued, claiming that this interpretation of the uniform rule infringed unduly on his right to religious expression.[59] Writing on behalf of the court, Justice Rehnquist held:

> In the context of the present case, when evaluating whether military needs justify a particular restriction on religiously motivated conduct, courts must give great deference to the professional judgment of military authorities concerning the relative importance of a particular military interest. . . . Not only are courts

'ill-equipped to determine the impact upon discipline that any particular intrusion upon military authority might have,' but the military authorities have been charged by the Executive and Legislative Branches with carrying out our Nation's military policy.[60]

The Air Force did not have to explain its policy, let alone justify it. Nor was this a question of deference to congressional will; the Air Force had simply issued and interpreted its own regulation without the notice and comment that other governmental agencies must undergo prior to issuing regulations. Captain Goldman had either to remove his yarmulke or leave the service, just as every other Orthodox Jew and Sikh in the service would have to do. Rehnquist's revolution was complete. No longer would the personnel policies of the Armed Forces of the United States be subjected to any meaningful constitutional review. He had separated military society from civil society and from constitutionally protected rights. Mazur argues that in this separate sphere, conservatives proceeded to institutionalize their prejudices about homosexuals,[61] women,[62] religious minorities,[63] and even law students[64] in ways that make the military less strong[65] and America less equitable.

Separate is seldom equal. As noted above, Mazur emphasizes the role that Justice Rehnquist and the Supreme Court played in the separation of military personnel from American society.[66] Having established that claim, she moves on to argue that Rehnquist's views about the separate nature of the armed services—while not necessarily accurate when he penned them—contributed to their self-fulfillment.[67] Ten years after the *Goldman* decision, a former Vice Chief of Naval Operations observed, "The armed forces are no longer representative of the people they serve. More and more, enlisted [men and women] as well as officers are beginning to feel that they are special, better than the society they serve." [68] He added that this "is not healthy in an armed force serving a democracy."[69] This sense of superiority reached near-critical levels in the late-1990s. Since the war in Afghanistan started in late 2001, however, the sense of crisis has greatly subsided, even if the separation and feelings of superiority have not. Mazur argues that the separate sphere gives the political leaders of government innumerable opportunities for mischief, space in which to employ questionable policies. The "military is the most respected and trusted institution, public or private,[70] within our society,"[71] and our elected representatives are not. Mazur argues that this fact may explain support for military detention and trials of accused terrorists. She views the military's autonomy as a factor contributing to the ill-advised policies or practices related to detention, interrogation, and trial of persons considered dangerous adversaries in the so-called "War on Terror."[72]

As will be discussed below, Bruce Ackerman goes further. He argues that an untethered military — with independent sources of political strength — may contribute to a constitutional crisis with even more far-reaching consequences.[73] Ackerman speculates that it may put the Chairman of the Joint Chiefs in the position of deciding to end a contested election and placing the opposing candidate in the White House.

The Soldier and the Republic.

Let us turn now to Ackerman's more wide-ranging book, one that also inquires how the people of the

18

United States relate to the members of the military sworn to support and defend their Constitution. In Mazur's book, the military is characterized as playing an oddly passive role in a campaign waged by social conservatives outside the services to carve out a separate sphere. In important contrast, Bruce Ackerman's book posits military leaders playing a more active role in reshaping the American political order. His account ascribes to senior military leaders a role that is less central to the narrative but more decisive in the outcome. Ackerman is a Sterling Professor of Law and Political Science at Yale, one of the university's most distinguished chairs. He earned this honor in great part because of his prolific record of high-impact scholarship, having written dozens of books and articles on economic and civil rights, constitutionalism, and jurisprudence, and, more recently, on national security.[74] Drawing on this extensive background, Ackerman delivered the prestigious 2010 Tanner Lectures on Human Values at Princeton University and subsequently published these lectures as *The Decline and Fall of the American Republic*.[75]

The book's title, of course, echoes the tropes made famous by the works of two British historians: *The History of the Decline and Fall of the Roman Empire,* the 18th-century classic by Edward Gibbon, and, less directly, the "Rise and Fall" discourse so famously articulated by Ackerman's colleague at Yale, historian Paul M. Kennedy.[76] These historical discourses are sophisticated, nuanced, and ultimately pessimistic—ending inevitably with a fall. Gibbon's classic attributed the decline and fall of the Roman Empire to its decadent civil society and poor leadership, which abdicated responsibility for the defense of the realm to mercenaries.

Public virtue, which among the ancients was denominated as patriotism, is derived from a strong sense of our own interest in the preservation and prosperity of the free government of which we are members. Such a sentiment, which had rendered the legions of the Roman republic almost invincible, could make but a very feeble impression on the mercenary servants of a despotic prince; it became necessary to supply that defect by other motives, different but no less compulsory — honor and religion.[77]

The mercenaries eventually turned on Rome, Gibbon explained, destroying the world's greatest power and condemning Europe to centuries of darkness. While drawn from immense scholarship, Gibbon's history was also shaped by the urgent issues of the time in which he wrote. The American Revolution raged, and London relied increasingly on Hessian mercenaries in the long struggle to retain the North American colonies.[78] To some extent, Gibbon's history of ancient Rome naturally reflected his views on the state of the contemporary British Empire.

Britain lost a second empire 200 hundred years later. Born in 1945 and writing some 40 years after that, British-born historian Paul Kennedy posited that great empires overreach and consequently collapse under the unbearable combined weight of far-flung military obligations and unsustainable domestic consumption.[79] For Kennedy, as for Gibbon, the responsibility for a great power's decline typically lies in ill-considered grand strategy or, more specifically, in the failure of that society's leaders to make the tough choices necessary for allocating resources to sustain vital institutions.[80] "Rise and Fall" studies inevitably correlate the vigor of society's with the extent to which their leaders' decisions are virtuous. These studies exhibit an essentially historicist way of explaining the world. They focus on where things went wrong and how conscious (and contingent) human decisions shaped destiny. Many other scholars would, of course, attribute national or imperial decline to exogenous factors, such as ill-tempered gods, uncontrollable plagues, drinking water pipes made of deadly lead, or foreign invaders led by generals of unique genius.[81] But for members of the "School of Decline," the fault lies not in our stars, but in ourselves.

Applying this formula to examine the troubles of today's great power,[82] Ackerman argues that the United States has started its decline, and that it will fall. Whereas for Kennedy, the word "fall" signifies a relative loss of economic and military power, for Ackerman it means a loss of a republic's virtue, the demise of the very characteristic that defines the society, gives it integrity, and makes it strong. Ackerman grimly predicts in one breathless paragraph:

(1) [T]he evolving system of presidential nominations will lead to the election of an increasing number of charismatic outsider types who gain office by mobilizing activist support for extremist programs of the left or right; (2) all presidents, whether extremist or mainstream, will rely on media consultants to design streams of sound bites aimed at narrowly segmented micropublics, generating a politics of unreason that will often dominate public debate; (3) they will increasingly govern through their White House staff of superloyalists, issuing executive orders that their staffers will impose on the federal bureaucracy even when they conflict with congressional mandates; (4) they will engage with an increasingly politicized military in ways that may greatly expand their effective power to put their executive orders into force throughout the nation; (5) they will legitimate their unilateral actions

through an expansive use of emergency powers, and (6) assert "mandates from the People" to evade or ignore congressional statutes when public opinion polls support decisive action; (7) they will rely on elite lawyers in the executive branch to write up learned opinions that vindicate the Constitutionality of their most blatant power grabs. These opinions will publicly rubber-stamp presidential actions months or years before the Supreme Court gets into the act . . . [w]ith . . . the president's media machine generating a groundswell of support for his power grab, the Supreme Court may find it prudent to stage a strategic retreat, allowing the president to displace Congress and use his bureaucracy and military authority to establish a new regime of law and order.[83]

This is his outline and argument. In short, Ackerman predicts an executive coup made partially possible by a politicized and anti-democratic military.

While he assembles an argument that explains some serious problems, his conclusions sometimes seem overreaching. Ackerman reads widely and frequently spots subterranean trends before others; but in this instance, he may have over-learned the lessons from his principal case studies. Specifically, Ackerman rests his argument on the lessons he draws from three recent crises in the recent American constitutional experience: Watergate, Iran-Contra, and the so-called "War on Terror." While Ackerman refers to the scandals of the early-1970s and mid-1980s throughout this book, it seems that he would not have written it without the outrageous "Torture Memos" issued by the Justice Department's Office of Legal Counsel in the summer of 2002.[84] Ackerman rests much of his argument on the claim that the "'torture memos' do not represent a momentary aberration but a symptom of deep structural pathologies that portend worse abuses in the future."[85]

With the scandalous "Torture Memos" as his principal source of inspiration, Ackerman ascribes the loss of republican values to the "transformation of the White House into a platform for charismatic extremism and bureaucratic lawlessness."[86] Ackerman does not foresee a decline in the nation's morality or its democratic processes. He expects America to continue to develop into a more moral nation and to continue to hold regular elections. He does, however, predict that the duly elected Presidents will govern radically and without adequate checks from Congress or the Judiciary.[87] In Ackerman's dark interpretation of the emerging "administrative Presidency," the United States will come to be governed through a largely unaccountable executive branch.[88] Presidents will set policy by edict and implement it through the burgeoning White House staff rather than through the executive departments or agencies. These unaccountable Presidents will determine policy on their own or through czars who have not faced the confirmation process. They will establish the policies through decrees, executive orders, executive agreements, administrative rules, interpretations, or signing statements. "Superloyalist" lawyers in the Office of Legal Counsel at the Justice Department or the White House Counsel will provide self-proving legal support for these policies. Pollsters and spinmasters will hone the public messages. Thousands of political appointees will implement them.[89] The Presidents will enjoy the tacit consent of a fragmented Congress and an excessively deferential judiciary. In each of Ackerman's scenarios, the military plays a critical role. In the direst of these, "the military will operate as a power behind the throne."[90]

One of Ackerman's most compelling concerns is the increasingly politicized and autonomous military.[91] This three-part argument notes first that the Chairman of the Joint Chiefs has become an unelected political force of his own. Second, the "military colonization" over national security decisionmaking has been supported by the ever-increasing number of officers and retired officers obtaining high-level civilian appointments. Third, and possibly fatally, these two premises have been reinforced because military professionals have become more political and partisan. In short, Ackerman posits that the officer corps, which over time has increasingly identified with the conservative wing of American politics, may resolve some future political crisis by handing the presidency to the Republican candidate on the basis that only by doing so could a security catastrophe be prevented (discussed below).[92]

First, Ackerman explains that since the passage of the Goldwater-Nichols Department of Defense Reorganization Act of 1986, the Chairman of the Joint Chiefs has enjoyed an increasingly autonomous and powerful status as the unified voice speaking on behalf of the Armed Forces.[93] Charismatic chairmen, such as Colin Powell and Michael Mullen, have been able to pursue policy objectives by appealing directly to the public, to the House or Senate leadership, and to the executive. Thus, they may have sometimes outmaneuvered their civilian defense secretaries and even Presidents in contests to shape military policy.[94] For example, Ackerman claims, that because he enjoyed a significant autonomous power base, General Powell was able to foist on President Clinton his eponymous strategic doctrine amplifying the earlier Weinberger doctrine, *inter alia* limiting interventions to circumstances in which the United States could exert overwhelming force.[95] This maneuver, in Ackerman's view, left the elected leadership with a less meaningful ability to shape national security policy.

Secondly, Ackerman argues that career officers have colonized the key positions of the nominally civilian leadership of the military and paramilitary institutions, in the DoD, the National Security Council (NSC), and the intelligence community. Prior to 1980, the civilian leadership within the DoD was overwhelmingly nonmilitary; only 17 percent of these officials had as much as 5 years of military service.[96] Since 1980, the numbers have changed considerably. Nearly a quarter of them have had 15 years of service, and 44 percent have had 5 years.[97] Why is this shift problematic? First, having spent so much time in military careers, these officials are imbued with military culture and military views. Such views are neither wrong nor inferior, but they are frequently different from the civilian perspectives that are supposed to be setting policy. Likewise, those with a military background may have bureaucratic advantages (for instance, communicating with people in uniform in ways that enable them to connect better) that give them a bureaucratic-operational advantage over true civilians—particularly in an era in which the civilian appointments turn over so rapidly and take so long to fill.[98]

Ackerman also notes with concern the significant increase in the incidence of military professionals leading other security-related institutions such as the NSC and intelligence agencies.[99] For 4 decades following the establishment of the position in 1947, civilians served as National Security Advisor. Particularly in the years following President John Kennedy's appointment of McGeorge Bundy, heavyweights such as Walt W. Rostow, Henry Kissinger, and Zbigniew Brzezinski provided meaningful civilian control of the national security establishment. Ackerman further asserts that President Ronald Reagan's unfortunate appointments of Marine Colonel Robert "Bud" McFarlane and then Vice Admiral John Poindexter resulted in the Iran-Contra scandal. He cites Ivo Daalder and I. M. Destler, who note that Reagan's preferred choice, James A. Baker, would probably have exercised the common sense and the administrative skill needed to prevent the fiasco.[100] Even after the scandal threatened to bring down his administration, Reagan turned to another military officer, Colin Powell, and then President George H. W. Bush similarly appointed Army Lieutenant General Brent Scowcroft. The trend has only continued to intensify, as Presidents have since appointed career officers to chair the NSC,[101] to hold key posts in the Central Intelligence Agency (CIA),[102] and, more recently, to serve as Directors of National Intelligence.[103] Ackerman makes this point cogently:

> A similar pattern prevails at the Defense Department. Its recent decision to create an undersecretary of defense for intelligence is a big deal — the new office ranks just behind the reliably civilian undersecretary [sic] in the department's pecking order. But only the first incumbent was a civilian [Stephen Cambone], and he has been followed by a retired three-star general [James Clapper, U.S. Air Force]. If this military turn continues, the undersecretary will not function as a civilian check on the enormous intelligence operations run by the department's Defense Intelligence Agency or its National Security Agency — both under the leadership of active-duty three-stars. He will be looking at the world through the same professional prisms as his subordinates. When he leaves the Pentagon to talk with the president's new director of national intelligence [Admiral Dennis Blair], the conversation will continue in the same vein — so long as the director is

a military man, one retired three-star general will be talking to another retired three-star. And if they get together to give the president advice, he undoubtedly will want to hear the opinion of his four-star national security advisor [Retired Marine Corps General James L. Jones].[104]

Ackerman's point here is very important: the nation does not have meaningful civilian control over the military intelligence apparatus if its civilian leaders are retired generals.[105] Even though the overwhelming majority of intelligence activities, personnel, and funding are military, the intelligence process retains fundamental political dimensions, and therefore requires civilian input.[106] Relying on a relatively homogeneous military community to lead intelligence activities deprives decisionmakers of other valuable perspectives.

Ackerman's snapshot may not be quite as predictive as he fears. In the year following Ackerman's writing of this passage, President Barack Obama has appointed civilians to succeed military men in the positions of Under Secretary of Defense for Intelligence (Michael Vickers) and National Security Advisor (Thomas E. Donilon).[107] Today, only one of the top 15 people on the NSC staff has significant military experience. Moreover, command responsibilities continue to require that the directors of the Defense Intelligence Agency (DIA) and the National Security Agency be uniformed officers, indicating that Congress has deemed appointment of officers to these positions as necessary for the agencies' success.[108] Likewise, Ackerman found "14 of 29 key positions" in the Obama DoD were held by retired officers.[109] My own survey (approximately a year later) finds 15 of 92 appointments at the level of Deputy Assistant Secretary or above were held by retired military. Of these 15 retired officers, more than half direct units administering personnel or military community and family affairs (including reserve and prisoner-of-war affairs) for which the leadership of veterans seems uniquely appropriate. Likewise, the service departments of the Army, Navy, and Air Force do have a higher proportion of senior administrators with significant military experience, which also makes good sense — given their mission to organize, train, and equip military personnel. On the other hand, civilians dominate in DoD's most politically sensitive strategy and policy positions.

Over the past several decades, in addition to taking on new and more politically oriented roles in the government, individual officers have become more politicized and partisan. First of all, they are voting. Prior to World War II, "[t]he overwhelming majority of officers even refused to vote, since it required them to think of themselves as partisans for the time it took to cast a secret ballot."[110] By 1944, however, a quarter of senior officers voted in the presidential election.[111] Since then, political participation became common. The Reagan Revolution brought another dramatic change. In the late-1970s, over half of all higher-ranking officers identified themselves as political independents and only a third as Republicans.[112] In 1984, over half self-identified as Republicans, a portion that rose to two-thirds in 1996 — at which point only 7 percent were Democrats.[113] Mazur also notes the increasing levels of partisanship, citing as support a statement made by a West Point professor and a speech given by Secretary of Defense Robert Gates at the Air Force and Naval Academy graduations in 2007.[114] Because the current officer corps is also more likely than not to believe it acceptable to advocate publicly for specific military policies,[115] civilian control is diminished—particularly if that civilian is viewed as soft on national defense.

Ackerman discusses possible implications of having an officer corps that overwhelmingly favors one party over another. Here he echoes Gibbon's account of the fall of Rome. He identifies several hypothetical scenarios in which the constitutional order faces critical but not implausible challenges. One such scenario involves a highly contested election à la *Bush v. Gore,* in which the Supreme Court demurs from deciding this "political question," even as the crisis continues past Inauguration Day, (much as it threatened to do in 1876-77 and again in 2000).[116] Finally, the Chairman of the Joint Chiefs steps in and calls a halt to the chaos in the name of national security.[117] He declares the conservative to be the winner, based on his reading of polling data (not votes in the Electoral College), which finds that candidate more popular. Ackerman does not seem as exorcised by this hypothetical intervention itself as he is by the dangerous precedent it sets for further military meddling in the constitutional order.[118] His other hypotheticals also involve some form of military participation in their resolution.[119]

After painting the disturbing crises that might impend, Ackerman proposes a variety of constructive institutional solutions to ensure that the White House and the military reconnect more faithfully with the constitutional order that has sustained the republic for more than 2 centuries. First, he proposes a raft of arrangements to improve the functioning of the democratic process. To reduce the likelihood of electing demagogues to the presidency, he revives his proposal for a national "Deliberation Day."[120] To ensure that serious journalists continue to perform watchdog functions, he would create the "Internet news voucher" and a "National Endowment for Journalism."[121] To avoid another contested electoral crisis, Ackerman supports the Popular Sovereignty Initiative, an interstate pact in which states commit their Electoral College votes to whichever candidate earns the most popular votes.[122]

Then Ackerman offers a more radical set of organizational adjustments intended to halt the march of the "institutional presidency" and restore the rule of law. First, Ackerman would establish a Supreme Executive Tribunal composed of nine judges appointed to long but staggered terms and subject to confirmation by the Senate.[123] This tribunal would review the legal opinions made by the White House Counsel and the Department of Justice's Office of Legal Counsel in an effort to hammer out consensual positions on questions related to executive authority.[124] As part of a grand bargain restructuring the separation of powers among the branches of government, Ackerman would also reform the Senate's filibuster rules to ensure that presidential appointments receive up or down votes.[125]

Among Ackerman's many reform proposals, and most important for our purposes, is his recommendation to draft and adopt a new Canon of Military Ethics, aimed at reinvigorating the principle of civilian control.[126] Ackerman hopes that a Presidential Commission on Civil-Military Relations would undertake several years of study to shape a realistic code of conduct. Once drafted, Congress would enact it, or the President could order it into effect.[127] At first blush, this proposal seems facile. The principle of civilian control of the military is clearly important and relatively noncontroversial as far as principles go, but what does it mean? Ackerman does not really answer, but would hand this question to the Presidential Commission. Given the diverse social, political, cultural, technical, and administrative issues involved, Ackerman may be correct. Perhaps ordinary political processes cannot resolve such a complex set of problems, and a Commission is required.

To support necessary changes, Ackerman also offers a few more specific proposals. He would pass a new emergency powers law that requires increased levels of congressional involvement as security crises continue.[128] He would amend the Goldwater-Nichols legislation so that the Chairman of the Joint Chiefs no longer has a statutory seat on the NSC; he or she would attend meetings only at the invitation of the Secretary of Defense or the President.[129] Ackerman would extend civilian experience requirements beyond the top echelons of the DoD. Currently the Secretary and Deputy Secretary of Defense must spend, respectively, 10 and 7 post-uniformed years as civilians before they can be appointed.[130] The service secretaries must spend at least 5 years as civilians.[131] The Under Secretary of Defense for Policy must also come from civilian life, although no specific time requirement is imposed.[132] Ackerman would extend this mechanism more broadly within the DoD and to the National Security Advisor and Director of National Intelligence.

While I applaud the effort to encourage Presidents to reach beyond the military to find their civilian leaders, this particular fix seems somewhat ill tailored. After 20 or 30 years in the military, individuals are not likely to dramatically change their mindsets by spending 5 years working for a defense contractor or doing defense-related work in academia. If they have been working for 5 years in a field completely unrelated to the military, their relevant skills and interest in military affairs may have diminished significantly. At the risk of being one of those reviewers who writes about what he would include in the book rather than what *is* included, I wish that Ackerman had instead focused some attention on what influential educational and civic institutions could do to educate future military and civilian leaders to make wiser decisions.[133] As these institutions invest more in this kind of education, their graduates seem more likely to receive leadership appointments — and to fulfill their roles wisely.

What Kind of Civil-Military Relationship Do We Want?

These two important books raise troubling questions about the relationship between America's Armed Forces and the wider society. Both point to the isolation of the military from broader society and discuss the significant risks that this isolation creates. But neither goes far enough in examining what we should expect from that relationship. In general terms, the wish list has not changed in decades. First, military officers should do as they are directed by the National Command Authority in the legitimate pursuit of national security and related objectives. Second, military personnel should act publicly in a politically neutral way. Third, the Armed Forces should be appropriately equipped and adequately trained to complete their assigned tasks. Fourth, their leaders should provide civilian leadership with the appropriate military capabilities needed to protect the nation and execute national policy. These axioms remain valid as far as they go, but, as Mazur and Ackerman observe, much else has changed. Mazur focuses on the military culture, which has evolved dramatically since the end of the draft, mostly in ways that further distanced it from the wider society. Ackerman focuses on changes in the constitutional order—in our polity—that portend for the military a new role as power broker. Both authors offer some laudable suggestions for how to improve the relationship between the military and civil society.

The end of the draft and the rise of the modern military-industrial state inevitably changed the range of possibilities for civil-military relations. An institutionalized volunteer military has supplanted the nation's long reliance on citizen-soldiers. The implications of this change for the nation are myriad. For example, the military is now composed of a less representative sample of Americans—volunteers as opposed to draftees. American society is thus composed of a smaller portion of people with military experience, since volunteer regulars generally serve longer than draftees on 2-year tours. This has led to a growing gap in mutual understanding between the military and civil sectors. Likewise, fewer of our elected leaders have military experience, which would give them personal insight into war and the military—and the credibility to make decisions contrary to the advice of military professionals.

Half a century ago, outgoing President Dwight D. Eisenhower presciently warned against the distractions imposed by the military-industrial complex on the "diligent in pursuit of the Nation's great goals."[134]

> In the councils of government, we must guard against the acquisition of unwarranted influence, whether sought or unsought, by the military-industrial complex. The potential for the disastrous rise of misplaced power exists and will persist.

We must never let the weight of this combination endanger our liberties or democratic processes. We should take nothing for granted. Only an alert and knowledgeable citizenry can compel the proper meshing of the huge industrial and military machinery of defense with our peaceful methods and goals, so that security and liberty may prosper together.[135]

Despite Eisenhower's admonitions, the cluster of interests representing members of Congress and their financial supporters, the military services, universities, think tanks, and the defense industries has dramatically reshaped the nation's political, research, economic, and strategic landscapes. I see no way to unravel that complex as long as the military needs specialized weapons, logistics, and communications systems. So we need more sophisticated tools and theories for controlling these interests and managing the conflicts of interest.

Yes, domestic factors and the choices leaders make do matter a great deal. In the tradition of British historians of empire, Edward Gibbon and Paul Kennedy, American constitutional law professors Bruce Ackerman and Diane Mazur offer explanations of the decline of civil-military relations that rely on internal factors. For a more complete and possibly more problematic understanding, however, we should also examine the external factors that contribute to reshaping the relationships between the armed forces and general society. In great part, civil-military relations have changed because of the end of the Cold War, the revolutionary ubiquity of information technology, and the rise in importance of nonstate actors, most notably of al Qaeda.

First, since the end of the Cold War released state and nonstate actors from the constraints of the superpower rivalry, conflict has proliferated. As a result, the United States has experienced a militarization of foreign relations. The increased resources invested in diplomacy, public diplomacy, and nonmilitary foreign aid pale in comparison to the proliferation of DoD relations with foreign governments, the influence of Regional Combatant Commands, and the impact of military assistance programs.[136] Even without wartime supplemental financing, the DoD budget is over 30 times greater than that of the State Department.[137] The DoD consists of approximately 1,400,000 service members on Active Duty, 860,000 Reserve and National Guard, and 790,000 civilians on installations in the United States and around the world.[138] The Department of State has approximately 29,000 employees.[139] With far greater resources than the State Department dispersed over far-flung locations, the DoD plays ever-more-diverse roles in U.S. foreign relations. Many of the changes blur the lines between the roles and missions traditionally deemed military and those viewed as diplomatic or political.

Second, the Information Revolution is constantly blurring the lines between civil and military capacities, issues, and campaigns. Cyberthreats and cyberwarfare can be conducted by military or civilian authorities and against states, nonstate entities, or individuals. Likewise, unmanned aerial vehicles are being operated by military and nonmilitary organizations, often with operationally indistinguishable missions. Global information systems and highly flexible drones erase many of the distinctions between the military and civilian spheres. These new technologies irrevocably smudge the lines between war and peace.

The war against al Qaeda has rapidly accelerated the breakdown between civil and military spheres because the United States has been fighting a "war" with a nonstate actor. The National Command Authority is constantly deciding whether to employ military or civilian assets in combating al Qaeda. For example, the U.S. President now possesses dramatically expanded powers to order the killing of an individual outside a traditional war zone. The law has been hard pressed to keep up with these developments. The nature of the enemy (nonstate, transnational), the tools available (weapons, cyber media, diplomacy, public affairs), and the laws and norms applicable (humanitarian, human rights, domestic, privacy, and secrecy laws) all shape the landscape in ways that inevitably alter civil-military relations. If this is emblematic of an epoch in which sovereignty itself is in decline, then it will not be repaired with the demise of al Qaeda.

Diane Mazur and Bruce Ackerman's new books make important contributions to the dialogue, reminding us that a healthy relationship between civil society and the military matters for the nation's security and governance. Such a relationship does not emerge inevitably from some natural law of war and peace or intrinsic characteristics of civilian and military, let alone immutable, principles defining their interrelationships.[140] We must constantly evaluate these relationships to preserve essential values in the face of revolutionary change. The piecemeal and episodic decisions made by public authorities, such as Justice Rehnquist or President Obama, have tremendous and sometimes unseen cumulative significance. So, too, do global trends far beyond their control. Perhaps the most valuable contribution Professors Mazur and Ackerman make is to reframe and restart a national discussion about the relationship between our national security apparatus and our republic.

ENDNOTES

1. The U.S. National Security Strategy articulates a similar list in explaining the importance of promoting democracy abroad by working to strengthen "key institutions of democratic account-ability—free and fair electoral processes, strong legislatures, civilian control of militaries, honest police forces, independent and fair judiciaries, a free and independent press, a vibrant private sector, and a robust civil society." The White House, *The National Security Strategy of the United States of America*, Washington, DC, 2010, p. 37, available from *www.whitehouse.gov/sites/default/files/rss_viewer/national_security_strategy.pdf*.

2. Surprisingly few scholars have attempted significant studies of the civil-military relationship in the United States. To the author's knowledge, no one has completed a more thorough examination of civil-military relations since Samuel P. Huntington published his magisterial work, *The Soldier and the State*, in 1957. See Samuel P. Huntington, *The Soldier and the State: The Theory and Politics of Civil-Military Relations*, Cambridge, MA: Belknap Press of Harvard University Press, 1957; see also Deborah N. Pearlstein: "The Soldier, the State, and the Separation of Powers," *Texas Law Review*, Vol. 90, 2012 (providing an extensive review of the literature and analyzing the ways in which professional military advice does, does not, and can better conform to separation of powers theory); and Morris Janowitz, *The Professional Soldier: A Social and Political Portrait*, New York, NY: The Free Press, 1971.

3. See David Kirkpatrick, "Military Backs New Leaders in Tunisia," *The New York Times*, January 16, 2011, p. A4; CNN, "Ousted Tunisian Strongman Convicted of Corruption Charges," June 20, 2011, available from *articles.cnn.com/2011-06-20/world/tunisia.ben.ali_1_corruption-charges-abidine-ben-ali-tunisians?_s=PM:WORLD*.

4. See, e.g., Larisa Epatko, "What is the Role of the Military in Egypt's Transition?" *The Rundown, PBS NewsHour*, February 7, 2011, available from *www.pbs.org/newshour/rundown/2011/02/egypt-military.html*.

5. See David Kirkpatrick, "Military Flexes Its Muscles as Islamists Gain in Egypt," *The New York Times*, December 8, 2011, p. A6.

6. See, e.g., Zoltan Barany: "The Role of the Military," *Journal of Democracy*, Vol. 22, No. 4, October 2011, pp. 31-34.

7. See, e.g., *ibid.*, pp. 28-31.

8. Oath of Office, 5 U.S.C. § 3331, 2006. The oath taken by National Guard officers also includes support and defense of the state's constitution and obedience to its governor. Appointment Oath, 32 U.S.C. § 312, 2006.

9. Chairman of the Joint Chiefs of Staff, *The National Military Strategy of the United States of America 2011: Redefining America's Military Leadership*, Washington, DC: Joint Chiefs of Staff, 2011, available from *www.jcs.mil//content/files/2011-02/020811084800_2011_NMS_-_08_FEB_2011.pdf*.

10. Contrast *ibid.* with Chairman of the Joint Chiefs of Staff, *The National Military Strategy of the United States of America: A Strategy for Today; A Vision for Tomorrow*, Washington, DC: Joint Chiefs of Staff, 2004, available from *www.defense.gov/news/mar2005/d20050318nms.pdf*.

11. Admiral Michael Mullen, Chairman of the Joint Chiefs of Staff, Commencement Address at the U.S. Military Academy, May 21, 2011, available from *www.jcs.mil/speech.aspx?ID=1598*.

12. For other examples of this kind of high-profile reminder, see Secretary of Defense Robert M. Gates's admonition that as officers, "you will have a responsibility to communicate to those below you that the American military must be non-political," as delivered in graduation speeches in 2007 at the U.S. Naval Academy, Annapolis, MD, and at the U.S. Air Force Academy, Colorado Springs, CO. Robert M. Gates, Secretary of Defense, Commencement Address at the U.S. Naval Academy, May 25, 2007, available from *www.defense.gov/speeches/speech.aspx?speechid=1154*; *idem*, Commencement Address at the U.S. Air Force Academy, May 30, 2007, available from *www.defense.gov/speeches/speech.aspx?speechid=1157*; see also Admiral Michael Mullen, "From the Chairman: Military Must Stay Apolitical," *Joint Forces Quarterly*, Issue 50, Third Quarter, 2008, p. 2 (reminding the members of the Armed Services to remain apolitical in an essay published during the 2008 U.S. presidential campaign).

13. See University of Florida Levin School of Law, "Faculty and Staff: Diane H. Mazur," available from *www.law.ufl.edu/faculty/mazur/*.

14. Michael F. Shaughnessy, Interview with Diane H. Mazur, *Education News*, November 9, 2010, available from *www.educationnews.org/commentaries/102607.htm*.

15. *Ibid.*

16. Diane H. Mazur, *A More Perfect Military: How the Constitution Can Make Our Military Stronger*, New York: Oxford University Press, 2010, p. 5.

17. *Ibid.,* p. 13.

18. See generally *ibid.*

19. See, e.g., *ibid.,* pp. 120-126, 146-164, 174-180.

20. See generally *ibid.,* pp. 53-73.

21. *Ibid.* p. 88.

22. *Orloff v. Willoughby,* 345 U.S. 83 (1953), p. 91; see Mazur, pp. 42-45.

23. *Orloff,* 343 U.S., pp. 93-94 (emphasis added), notes that the military is governed by military law and military justice—a separate system of order and discipline—but not that it constitutes a separate society.

24. Mazur, p. 42.

25. William H. Rehnquist, "A Random Thought on the Segregation Cases," *Nomination of Justice William Hubbs Rehnquist: Hearings Before the Senate Committee on the Judiciary,* 99th Cong., 1986, p. 315, available from *www.gpoaccess.gov/congress/senate/judiciary/sh99-1067/browse.html*.

26. Mazur, p. 45, quotes Frank I. Michelman: "The Supreme Court 1985 Term—Forward: Traces of Self-Government," *Harvard Law Review,* Vol. 100, No. 4, 1986, pp. 4-77, especially p. 8.

27. Mazur, p. 45.

28. See *Flower v. United States,* 452 F.2d 80 (5th Cir. 1972), pp. 81-82, reversed 407 U.S. 197, 1972.

29. *Ibid.,* p. 82; Mazur, p. 46.

30. *Flower,* 452 F.2d, p. 91. Flower was convicted under 18 U.S.C. § 1382: "Whoever reenters or is found [within a military post] after having been removed therefrom or ordered not to re-enter by any officer or person in command or charge thereof— Shall be fined not more than $500 or imprisoned not more than six months, or both." *Ibid.,* p. 87 (internal quotation marks omitted).

31. *Flower,* 407 U.S. pp. 198-199, quotes *Jamison v. Texas,* 318 U.S. 413 (1943), p. 416.

32. *Ibid.,* pp. 200-201 (citations omitted).

33. See Mazur, p. 47.

34. 411 U.S. 677 (1973); see Mazur, p. 49.

35. *Frontiero,* 411 U.S., pp. 680-681; Mazur, p. 48.

36. *Frontiero,* 411 U.S., pp. 688, 690-691.

37. *Ibid.,* p. 690.

38. *Ibid.,* p. 691.

39. *Frontiero v. Laird,* 341 F. Supp. 201 (M.D. Ala. 1972), p. 206.

40. Mazur, pp. 48-49.

41. Rehnquist did not actually draft a dissenting opinion. The syllabus merely notes that he dissented by endorsing "the reasons stated by Judge [Richard] Rives in his opinion for the District Court." *Frontiero,* 411 U.S., p. 691.

42. *Parker v. Levy,* 417 U.S. 733 (1974); *Rostker v. Goldberg,* 453 U.S. 57 (1981); *Goldman v. Weinberger,* 475 U.S. 503 (1986).

43. Mazur, pp. 55-56.

44. *Ibid.,* p. 56.

45. *Ibid.*

46. *Ibid.,* p. 57, citations for Levy's public statement noted in *Parker,* 417 U.S., p. 737.

47. *Parker,* 417 U.S., pp. 736, 738.

48. Mazur, p. 59.

49. *Parker,* 417 U.S., p. 744, quotes Orloff v. Willoughby, 345 U.S. 83 (1953), p. 94.

50. See Mazur, p. 59; see also *Parker,* 417 U.S., pp. 744-745.

51. See Mazur, pp. 60-61.

52. See Proclamation No. 4771, 45 Fed. Reg. 45, 247 (July 2, 1980); see also Doug Bandow: "Draft Registration: The Politics of Institutional Immortality," *Cato Policy Analysis,* No. 214, August 15, 1994, available from *www.cato.org/pubs/pas/pa-214.html.*

53. See *Rostker v. Goldberg,* 453 U.S. 57 (1981), p. 59; see also Mazur, p. 62.

54. Mazur, pp. 64-65.

55. *Rostker,* 453 U.S., p. 67.

56. Mazur, p. 68.

57. See *ibid.,* p. 66.

58. See generally *Goldman v. Weinberger,* 475 U.S. 503, 1986.

59. See Mazur, pp. 69–72; *Goldman*, 475 U.S., pp. 504-505, quotes Air Force Regulation AFR 35-10, regarding Air Force Dress Code, 1-6.h(2)(f) (1980), "headgear will not be worn . . . [w]hile indoors except by armed security police in the performance of their duties."

60. *Goldman*, 475 U.S., pp. 507–508 (citations and internal quotation marks omitted).

61. See Mazur, pp. 146-154.

62. See *ibid.*, pp. 165-180.

63. See *ibid.*, pp. 69-173.

64. See *ibid.*, pp. 6-9. Mazur explains that ROTC programs left many university campuses because they would not comply with academic standards and because the end of the Selective Service made ROTC less popular, not, as was commonly held, because of any hostility on the part of elite universities. The inaccurate but prevailing story fed an unwarranted sense that military people were unwelcome in the wider society. See *ibid.* Similarly, she argues that Congress's threats to cut funding to higher education institutions that prohibit ROTC or prevent military recruitment on campus, otherwise known as the Solomon Amendment controversies, unnecessarily exacerbated a minor issue. See *Rumsfeld v. Forum for Academic and Institutional Rights* (FAIR), 547 U.S. 47 (2006), pp. 51-53. The military should not have discriminated against homosexuals in service. Law schools should not have banned military recruiters. Congress should not have retaliated with the Solomon Amendment threatening to cut off all government support of the universities. Law professors should have realized that their case to overturn the Solomon Amendment would not succeed because the Supreme Court would view it as a military personnel issue, not a free-speech issue. See generally *Rumsfeld*, 547 U.S. 47. Mazur argues that the ROTC and the Solomon Amendment controversies arose because the Supreme Court had deprived members of the armed forces of freedoms enjoyed by a more tolerant civil society. See generally Mazur, ch. 1.

65. See, generally, Mazur, ch. 8. Mazur ascribes one important facet of the military's fragility as arising out its unwillingness

to draw from a broader swath of society, posing significant constraints on its ability to recruit and retain suitable candidates. As one result of this situation, she argues, the military ends up overpaying enlisted personnel. See *ibid.*, pp. 140-143. Even so, the services are taking in a declining rate of high-school graduates and an increasing number of recruits requiring "moral waivers" on account of their records of felony and serious misdemeanor convictions. The services have had to issue thousands of these waivers, including for persons convicted of "aggravated assault, burglary, robbery, and in a few cases, for making terrorist threats." *Ibid.*, pp. 138-139. The services have also been recruiting more former gang members. See *ibid.*, pp. 139-140.

66. See, e.g., *ibid.*, pp. 89-91; see also Endnotes 15-57 above and accompanying text.

67. See *ibid.*, p. 90. See generally *ibid.*, ch. 6.

68. See Mazur, p. 77, quoting Stanley R. Arthur, "The American Military: Some Thoughts on Who We Are and What We Are," in Vincent Davis, ed., *Civil-Military Relations and the Not-Quite Wars of the Present and Future,* Carlisle, PA: Strategic Studies Institute, U.S. Army War College, 1996, pp. 12-19.

69. *Ibid.*

70. See, e.g., Donna Miles, "Military Takes Top U.S. Confidence Rankings," American Forces Press Service, June 28, 2011, available from *www.jcs.mil/newsarticle.aspx?ID=641.* The DoD reports these findings proudly and without editorial comment on the Chairman's webpage, *ibid.*:

> Forty-seven percent said they have a "great deal" of confidence in the military, the highest rating, and 31 percent reported "quite a lot" of confidence. That [total] rating [of 78 percent] was 14 percent higher than for the second-ranking institution, small business, and 22 percent higher than for the third-ranking institution, the police. Other organizations rankings, in descending order of high confidence, were: organized religion, 48 percent; the medical system, 39 percent; the U.S. Supreme Court, 37 percent; the presidency, 35 percent; the public schools, 34 per-

cent; the criminal justice system, 28 percent; newspapers, 28 percent; television news, 27 percent; banks, 23 percent; organized labor, 21 percent; big business, 19 percent; and health maintenance organizations, 19 percent. Congress received the lowest high-confidence ranking, at 12 percent.

71. See Mazur, pp. 3-4, citing Frank Newport, "Americans' Confidence in Congress at All-Time Low," *Gallup News Service*, June 21, 2007.

72. See Mazur, ch. 7.

73. See *infra* Part III.

74. See Yale Law School, "Bruce Ackerman," available from *www.law.yale.edu/faculty/BAckerman.htm*.

75. Bruce Ackerman, *The Decline and Fall of the American Republic*, Cambridge, MA: Harvard University Press, 2010.

76. See Edward Gibbon, *The History of the Decline and Fall of the Roman Empire*, J. B. Bury, ed., London, UK: Fred de Fau & Co., 1906 (originally published 1789); Paul M. Kennedy, *The Rise and Fall of British Naval Mastery*, Dublin, Ireland: Ashfield Press, 1986; see also *idem, The Rise and Fall of the Great Powers: Economic Change and Military Conflict from 1500 to 2000*, New York: Vintage Books, 1989.

77. Gibbon, p. 10.

78. See Harold E. Selesky, "Colonial America," in Michael Howard, George Andreopoulos, and Mark R. Shulman, eds., *The Laws of War: Constraints on Warfare in the Western World*, New Haven, CT: Yale University Press, 1994, pp. 59-86, 79-80.

79. See Kennedy, *British Naval Mastery*, pp. 347-349, attributing the decline of the British Empire to its having "numerous defence burdens and obligations, without the corresponding capacity to sustain them"; *idem, Great Powers*, pp. 44-55, ascribing the decline of the Hapsburg Empire to increasing military costs, overextension of the military, and failure to preserve the domestic economy.

80. See Kennedy, *British Naval Mastery*, pp. xiv-xvii; *idem, Great Powers*, pp. xv, 539-540.

81. See, e.g., Sergio Sabbatanti and Sirio Fiorino: "The Antonine Plague and the Decline of the Roman Empire," *Le Infezioni in medicina*, Vol. 17, No. 4, 2009, pp. 261-275, discussing the plague's impact on the Roman Empire; Saint Augustine, *The City of God*, Marcus Dods, trans., Boston, MA: Digireads.com Publishing, 2009, pp. 89-90. See generally A. Trevor Hodge, *Roman Aqueducts and Water Supply*, London, UK: Duckworth, 2002, discussing water supply in the Roman Empire; Peter Heather, *The Fall of the Roman Empire: A New History*, New York, Oxford University Press, 2005, attributing the decline to overwhelming barbarian invasions.

82. For more on the "decline school," see Robert D. Schulzinger, "Complaints, Self-Justifications, and Analysis: The Historiography of American Relations since 1996," in *America in the World: The Historiography of American Foreign Relations Since 1941*, Michael J. Hogan, ed., Cambridge, UK: Cambridge University Press, 1996, pp. 395-424, 421-423; and Peter Schmeisser, "Taking Stock: Is America in Decline?" *The New York Times Magazine*, April 17, 1988, available from *www.nytimes.com/1988/04/17/magazine/taking-stock-is-america-in-decline.html?pagewanted=all&src=pm*.

83. Ackerman, *The Decline and Fall of the American Republic*, pp. 9-10.

84. See generally Karen J. Greenberg and Joshua L. Dratel, eds., *The Torture Papers: The Road to Abu Ghraib*, New York: Cambridge University Press, 2005, compiling the legal memoranda that appear to justify torture and other cruel, inhumane, and degrading treatment of detainees.

85. Ackerman, *The Decline and Fall of the American Republic*, p. 95. Trevor Morrison, who served as an Associate White House Counsel to President Obama, takes on this claim directly as part of his review, arguing that Ackerman misconstrues institutional realities that generally do constrain executive behavior. See Trevor W. Morrison: "Constitutional Alarmism," *Harvard Law Review*, Vol. 124, No. 7, 2011, p. 1688-1750. "[Ackerman's] account of the current state of affairs is too often oversimplified or false, its attraction to institutional innovation too often blind to the workaday needs of government and insensitive to the costs of change.

Ultimately, the book deals too little with the reality of executive Constitutionalism to offer a credible appraisal of its performance or to propose serious ideas for its reform."

86. Ackerman, *The Decline and Fall of the American Republic,* p. 11.

87. *Ibid.,* p. 40.

88. Ackerman cites extensively the writings of Elena Kagan, who pointedly describes this emerging phenomenon as the "administrative Presidency." See *ibid.,* pp. 36-38. Ackerman notes that Kagan played a key role in developing this form of governance while serving in the White House under President Bill Clinton. See *ibid.* As a professor at Harvard Law School, she became one of the leading theorists of this concept. Kagan's most notable scholarly work acknowledged the dangers of this shift: "lawlessness — that Presidents, more than agency officials acting independently, tend to push the envelope when interpreting statutes." *Ibid.,* p. 37, quotes Elena Kagan: "Presidential Administration," *Harvard Law Review,* Vol. 114, No. 8, 2001, pp. 2245-2385, 2249 (internal quotation marks omitted). But, Ackerman also notes that Kagan concluded that the disadvantages of this lawlessness "are outweighed by the "president's unique claims to democratic legitimacy." Ackerman, *The Decline and Fall of the American Republic,* p. 37.

89. Ackerman points out that President Kennedy had 196 high-level positions to fill, each requiring U.S. Senate confirmation. President Clinton had 786, and President George W. Bush had 1,141. When combined with the key posts that do not require confirmation, the current President can make some 3,000 key appointments. *Ibid.,* p. 34.

90. *Ibid.,* p. 11.

91. See generally *ibid.,* ch. 2.

92. *Ibid.,* pp. 61-62, 78-79.

93. *Ibid.,* p. 49; see Goldwater-Nichols Department of Defense Reorganization Act of 1986, 10 U.S.C. §§ 151-155, 2006.

94. Ackerman, *The Decline and Fall of the American Republic*, pp. 49–56.

95. See *ibid.*, pp. 51, 56.

96. *Ibid.*, pp. 56-57.

97. *Ibid.*, p. 57.

98. According to the most recent data available, the average political appointee faces a confirmation process that takes 8-1/2 months and then serves only 11 to 20 months. Cheryl Y. Markum *et al.*, *Department of Defense Political Appointments: Positions and Process*, Santa Monica, CA: RAND Corporation, 2001, p. xi. Ackerman notes that between 1979 and 2003, positions requiring Senate confirmation were vacant some 25 percent of the time. See Ackerman, *The Decline and Fall of the American Republic*, p. 157, citing Anne Joseph O'Connell: "Vacant Offices: Delays in Staffing Top Agency Positions," *Southern California Law Review*, Vol. 82, No. 5, 2009, pp. 913-1000, 962-963.

99. See Ackerman, *The Decline and Fall of the American Republic*, pp. 57-58.

100. See *ibid.*, p. 57, citing Ivo Daalder and I. M. Destler, *In the Shadow of the Oval Office: Profiles of the National Security Advisors and the Presidents They Served – from JFK to George W. Bush*, New York: Simon & Schuster, 2009, pp. 148-149.

101. Ackerman may be overstating his case as far as the office of the National Security Advisor is concerned. Brent Scowcroft was the last military appointee, because neither Presidents Clinton nor George W. Bush appointed officers or former officers. President Obama's first appointee, retired Marine General James L. Jones, lasted less than 2 years and was replaced by a civilian lawyer with no military background, Thomas E. Donilon. See Ackerman, *The Decline and Fall of the American Republic*, pp. 57-58.

102. Both Presidents George W. Bush and Obama appointed two directors of the CIA; notably, each appointed one civilian and one active-duty general. President George W. Bush appointed civilian Porter Goss and General Michael Hayden, U.S. Air Force

(Ret.), while President Obama appointed civilian Leon Panetta and then General David Petraeus, U.S. Army (Ret.).

103. The Directors of National Intelligence have been: Ambassador John Negroponte (April 21, 2005–February 13, 2007), Vice Admiral John Michael McConnell, U.S. Navy (Ret.) (February 13, 2007–January 27, 2009), Admiral Dennis C. Blair, U.S. Navy (Ret.) (January 28, 2009–May 28, 2010), David C. Gompert (a Naval Academy graduate and long-time civilian employee of the DoD, Acting, May 28-August 5, 2010); and Lieutenant General James R. Clapper, U.S. Air Force (Ret.) (August 5, 2010 to the present).

104. Ackerman, *The Decline and Fall of the American Republic,* pp. 58–59 (citations omitted). The "sic" indicates that the Under Secretary for Intelligence follows in succession to the reliably civilian Deputy Secretary (not "undersecretary").

105. See *ibid.,* p. 59.

106. See Robert Jervis: "What's Wrong with the Intelligence Process?" *International Journal of Intelligence and Counterintelligence,* Vol. 1, No. 1, Summer 1986, pp. 28-41, 39-41; see also, e.g., Mark R. Shulman: "The Rise and Fall of American Naval Intelligence, 1882-1917," *Intelligence and National Security,* Vol. 8, No. 2, 1993, pp. 214-266, 214, providing a historical perspective on the politicization of the collection and analysis work of the Office of Naval Intelligence.

107. Under Secretary Vickers did have some military experience early in his career, but he quickly moved to the CIA and then other civilian positions. Moreover, the President traditionally does not appoint civilians to some of these positions. The Director of the Defense Intelligence Agency is a general officer, with duties to serve as military intelligence advisor to the Secretary and the Chairman of the Joint Chiefs and to command the Joint Functional Component Command for Intelligence, Surveillance and Reconnaissance. 50 U.S.C. § 403-5(b)(5), 2006. See Defense Intelligence Agency, "About DIA," available from *www.dia.mil/about.* Likewise, Congress requires that the Director of the National Security Agency be recommended jointly by the Secretary of Defense and the Director of National Intelligence, before

being appointed by the President (10 U.S.C. § 201, 2006 and Supp., 2009. He also serves as Commander of the U.S. Cyber Command. Apparently his deputy is always a civilian. See National Security Agency-Central Security Service, "Who Is the Head of NSA/CSS? Frequently Asked Questions About NSA," available from *www.nsa.gov/about/faqs/about_nsa.shtml.*

108. 10 U.S.C. § 201, 2006 and Supp., 2009.

109. Ackerman, *The Decline and Fall of the American Republic,* p. 162.

110. *Ibid.,* p. 61.

111. *Ibid.* (meaning colonels and general officers).

112. *Ibid.,* stating that 55 percent of higher-ranking officers identified themselves as independents in 1976, while 33 percent identified themselves as Republican.

113. *Ibid.* Reading the same materials, Mazur notes that the author of the survey believed that his data "may have understated the size of the partisan divide." Mazur, *A More Perfect Military,* p. 86.

114. *Ibid.,* p. 83. Ackerman cites a survey taken at West Point. Ackerman, *The Decline and Fall of the American Republic,* p. 62.

115. *Ibid.,* p. 62, citing Ole R. Holsti, "Of Chasms and Convergences," in Peter D. Feaver and Richard H. Kohn, eds., *Soldiers and Civilians: The Civil-Military Gaps and American National Security,* Cambridge, MA: MIT Press, 2001, pp. 19-21, reporting on the survey conducted by the Triangle Institute for Security Studies; James A. David, "Attitudes and Opinions Among Senior Military Officers and a U.S. Cross-Section, 1998-99," in Feaver and Kohn, eds., *Soldiers and Civilians,* p. 120. "[Sixty-five] percent of senior officers think it is OK to go public and advocate military policies they believe are in the best interests of the United States."

116. Ackerman, *The Decline and Fall of the American Republic,* pp. 76–78; see *Bush v. Gore,* 531 U.S. 98, 2000.

117. *Ibid.*, p. 79.

118. *Ibid.*, pp. 78–79.

119. Ackerman discusses two additional scenarios as well: "The Extremist Scenario" and "The Crisis Scenario." See *ibid.*, pp. 79–81, 81–83.

120. *Ibid.*, pp. 127–31. See generally Bruce Ackerman and James S. Fishkin, *Deliberation Day*, New Haven, CT: Yale University Press, 2004.

121. Ackerman, *The Decline and Fall of the American Republic*, p. 133, giving shared credit to his colleague Ian Ayres for the idea of the "Internet news voucher."

122. *Ibid.*, pp. 136-137.

123. *Ibid.*, p. 143.

124. *Ibid.*, p. 143-146.

125. *Ibid.*, p. 158-159.

126. *Ibid.*, p. 159-160.

127. *Ibid.*, p. 160-161.

128. *Ibid.*, pp. 168–74. Here Ackerman reprises his 2006 book, *Before the Next Attack*. See Bruce Ackerman, *Before the Next Attack: Preserving Civil Liberties in an Age of Terrorism*, New Haven, CT: Yale University Press, 2006.

129. Ackerman, *The Decline and Fall of the American Republic*, pp. 163-164.

130. 10 U.S.C. § 113(a) (2006) (Secretary of Defense); 10 U.S.C. § 132(a) (2006) (Deputy Secretary).

131. 10 U.S.C. § 8013(a)(2) (2006) (Air Force); 10 U.S.C. § 3013(a)(2) (2006) (Army); 10 U.S.C. § 5013(a)(2) (2006) (Navy).

132. 10 U.S.C. § 134(a) (2006); 10 U.S.C. § 135(a) (2006); 10 U.S.C. § 136(a) (2006); 10 U.S.C. § 137(a) (2006).

133. See, e.g., Yale University, "The Brady-Johnson Program in Grand Strategy," available from *iss.yale.edu/brady-john-son-program-grand-strategy-and-studies-grand-strategy-graduate-seminar*; David Burt, "Faculty Approve New ROTC Resolutions," *Yale Daily News*, May 5, 2011, available from *www.yaledailynews.com/news/2011/may/05/faculty-approve-new-rotc-resolutions/*.

134. President Dwight D. Eisenhower, "Farewell Address, January 17, 1961," in *Public Papers of the Presidents, Dwight D. Eisenhower*, Washington, DC: U.S. Government Printing Office, 1961, pp. 1035-1040; also available from *avalon.law.yale.edu/20th_century/eisenhower001.asp*.

135. *Ibid.*

136. The 2011 fiscal year budget for the Department of State was $16.4 billion (excluding foreign assistance), while the budget for the DoD was $548.9 billion. Office of Management and Budget, Executive Office of the President, *Budget of the United States Government, Fiscal Year 2011*, Washington, DC: U.S. Government Printing Office, 2010.

137. See *ibid.*

138. U.S. Department of Defense, *Agency Financial Report*, Washington, DC: U.S. Government Printing Office, 2010, pp. 8-9.

139. U.S. Department of State, *Agency Financial Report*, Washington, DC: U.S. Government Printing Office, 2010, pp. 7-8.

140. See Michael Howard, *The Invention of Peace: Reflections on War and International Order*, New Haven, CT: Yale University Press, 2000, p. 1, quotes Sir Henry Maine's observation that "[w]ar appears to be as old as mankind, but peace is a modern invention."

www.ingramcontent.com/pod-product-compliance
Lightning Source LLC
Chambersburg PA
CBHW070501290526
45790CB00003B/1054